Your Emotional Intelligence (EQ) is said to be -

10x more important for your Success than the IQ!

EMOTIONAL INTELLIGENCE (EQ)

7 HIGHLY EFFECTIVE TECHNIQUES

TO LEVERAGE YOUR SUCCESS

AND HAPPINESS IN LIFE!

TABLE OF CONTENT

Introduction

Conclusion

- A few words from the Author E.N. Richardson
- A few words from the publisher: be-to-ce _ publishing

- ©Copyright

INTRODUCTION

I want to thank you and congratulate you for downloading the book,

"EMOTIONAL INTELLIGENCE.
7 Self-Control and EQ-Secrets that will leverage your Happiness and Success in Life".

This book contains proven steps and strategies on how to increase your level of emotional intelligence along with your self-control. The following chapters have highly valuable information on:

- What emotional intelligence is and how it differs from intellectual intelligence;

- The role that a healthy emotional intelligence plays in achieving success in certain aspects of life;

- Steps on how you can attain better self-awareness and self-control when it comes to your actions and emotions;

- The difference between reacting and responding and how the latter can help you develop your sense of self-control better;

- Strategies for connecting with people better to gain a more nuanced understanding of what makes them tick;

- And much, much more!

Thanks again for downloading this book, I hope you enjoy reading. I am confident, that it will have a great positive impact on your future!

CHAPTER 1: OVERVIEW OF EQ
WHY IT IS SO IMPORTANT

There was a time when one's intellectual quotient (or IQ, as it is more commonly referred to) was considered to be everything.

IQ's that were upwards of 140 are considered to be of the superior kind, so educational systems invested in all sorts of tests and programs that aimed to increase a student's IQ test scores.

Often, children who exhibited intelligence at an early age were placed in advanced classes or additional courses in order to foster their intellectual gifts.

Many of the world's greatest inventors and innovators certainly had the gift of a superior IQ.

Albert Einstein, the German genius renowned for his theory of relativity, and Thomas Edison, widely credited with the invention of the light bulb, are both known to possess formidable brain power, so to speak.

Yet for every Einstein or Edison who makes their mark on the world, there are hundreds or perhaps even thousands more genius-level IQ's who don't quite make the cut.

Some of them end up working for someone less intellectual than they are and quite a few end up as bums who while their life away on wasted talent. It seems that a superior IQ may not be a sure indicator of success, after all.

So, if IQ isn't everything, is there a kind of intelligence that has a greater bearing on your success and happiness? Apparently, there is. It is called "emotional intelligence" or EQ.

The concept of EQ can best be illustrated by the famous marshmallow test. In this experiment, a group of children aged 5 and below were placed in separate rooms.

A plate with a single marshmallow on it was set before each child. Before the supervising adult left the room, she told each child that they would be given another marshmallow if they left the one on the plate untouched until the adult returned.

The supervising adult then left the child alone with the marshmallow for about ten minutes.

A video camera had been set up beforehand to record the child's reactions while the supervising adult was out. A lot of the children could not resist eating the marshmallow and thus ended up having only one.

A few of the children, on the other hand, managed to refrain from eating the marshmallow on the plate in front of them and earned another one as a reward.

The experiment illustrates a couple of things about EQ. One is that it has got to do with self-control, motivation, and delayed gratification.

All of the children who participated knew that they would be rewarded with another marshmallow, but only a few of them were motivated enough to see the challenge through.

Another thing that you can observe from the experiment is that like with IQ, some individuals can possess a precocious EQ as well, with their propensity for discipline and motivation being quite evident at an early age.

But what exactly is Emotional Intelligence(EQ), and what sort of traits does it encompass?

In simpler terms, emotional intelligence is a person's ability to manifest the following:

1.) Motivation. This is an umbrella term that pertains to the mastery over one's emotions in order to commit to and work towards the accomplishment of one's personal goals.

2.) Self-awareness. Being able to recognize and understand how and why you feel and react to certain things is at the core of this trait.

3.) Empathy. Apart from having a keen understanding of your own feelings, a healthy EQ also entails being equally understanding of the emotions of other people in the same situation. This quality often makes it easier to relate to and deal with other people as a result.

4.) Self-management or self-control. Recognizing and acknowledging one's emotions, mood, reactions, and impulses are not enough. One must also be able to rein them in if the situation calls for it.

5.) Social skills. When you are able to control yourself and relate to others, you are more likely to work well with and possibly even lead other people. The ability to be a team player along with the capacity for resolving conflict also comes into play in this aspect.

So, how important is a good EQ towards achieving success? Very, it turns out that a healthy EQ is instrumental to accomplishing fulfillment in many key areas of life, such as:

1.) Leadership. A person with high emotional intelligence is better able to discern the needs of the people around him or her, whether in the workplace or in the family.

Understanding what motivates other people and being able to build strong bonds with them are what makes a leader effective in facilitating the emotional diversity of a group to make it function better as a cohesive whole rather than a fractured circle.

2.) Conflict resolution. The ability to empathize with and to understand what drives people's emotions.

This can not only help you to smooth any ruffled feathers but it can also enable you to see a conflict coming and thus take the necessary steps to prevent it.

Negotiating to come up with a win-win solution for all the parties involved also becomes easier when you are more in tune with the wants and needs of other people.

3.) Relationships. The strongest and most fulfilling relationships are often between people who are able to understand and relate to each other in an almost intuitive manner.

A strong EQ often means being aware of both yours and the other person's emotions and motivations, which in turn leads to a more open and constructive communication between both parties.

4.) Physical and mental health. Stress and anxiety wreak havoc on both the body and mind in the form of physical and mental illnesses.

Having a steady grip of your state of mind and being able to handle your own reactions to stress in a productive way can prevent a lot of stress or anxiety-related diseases or disorders.

People with higher EQ levels also tend to have a happier and more balanced outlook on life, and are thus less vulnerable to depressive mood swings.

5.) Overall success. The ability to delay immediate gratification in favor of a bigger goal helps you to increase your levels of self-confidence, focus on the task at hand, and to resist procrastination.

6.) Such a heightened level of internal motivation, coupled with the forging of strong bonds with others and the capacity to take on setbacks and to muster enough determination to push through, can only result in equally heightened levels of success in any field.

7.) The good news is that while quite a few people are born with a precocious EQ, just about anyone can train themselves to manifest the same traits as well.

The following chapters each feature particular steps that are all geared towards helping you become more motivated, empathetic, and in control of your own emotions and feelings.

It might take quite a bit of commitment as well as a few missteps along the way before you get to your ideal EQ level, but rest assured that both the destination and the journey will prove to be fulfilling in just about every sense.

So, go right ahead and turn the page to find out how you can start working towards your optimum self.

NOTES:

CHAPTER 2:
BE AWARE OF YOUR EMOTIONS

The first step towards a healthy EQ and a strong sense of self-control is awareness. You need to pay attention to your thoughts, feelings, and emotions and try to discern how such are formed within your mind.

The trouble with being mindful of your feelings and emotions nowadays is that you tend to operate in auto-pilot mode because of all the day to day demands that need tending.

So, in the process of rushing from one deadline to another and getting countless errands done in between, you tend to lose touch with your emotions and lose your sense of self as a result.

When you function on auto-pilot, you tend to react without much thought, so you lose valuable insight on what drives your actions and emotions.

The truth is that whenever you react to something or someone, you do so out of receiving either a reminder or information about another person, event, or situation.

You may be reacting in a certain way because of the situation itself, or because something about it reminds you about a deep-seated and unprocessed memory.

So, when you start to pay better attention to your emotions, you learn to trust them more and become a whole lot better at managing or harnessing them.

The following are just a handful of steps that you can do in everyday situations to become more mindful or your emotions and thus increase your EQ considerably:

1.) Never ignore your emotions or feelings, even if they don't necessarily feel good. Each emotion gives you a key insight into how your mind works and how it affects the way you behave. Do note that you do not (and should not, in many cases) have to act on your emotions. Simply acknowledge that they exist.

Do not pass judgment upon your emotions either, even on the bad ones like jealousy or anger. Ask yourself instead what that emotion is telling you about your current situation.

For example, if you feel very angry in the workplace or at home, is it because you feel as though your hard work is taken for granted or because you feel unfulfilled in some way?

2.) Whenever a feeling arises, try to analyze what triggered it. It would be helpful to give a name to that feeling or emotion or to connect it to a particular experience to help the process along.

For instance, if someone talks over you during a meeting or in a conversation, what is the first emotion that sweeps through you? Do you feel annoyed, irritated, or indifferent?

Conversely, pay attention to how you feel whenever someone compliments you on your work, your personality, or your appearance? Is the first emotion that you feel a burst of pride or gratitude?

Identify the proper emotion and name it accordingly, and then recognize what event or situation triggered it (e.g., being treated rudely makes you feel irritated while being complimented makes you feel proud and happy).

Recognize the physical manifestations of every emotion. While minds and bodies function differently, they do not do so separately and they often reflect each other's states.

Learning how to read and interpret your body's physical cues as they relate to your emotions help you become more self-aware.

If you have trouble recognizing an emotion's physical cues, you can jot down in a special journal how your body feels whenever you are experiencing a particular feeling.

For starters, tightness in the chest or knots along your shoulders can herald feelings of stress and anxiety while sadness can be described as a heaviness in your limbs or a reluctance to get up in the morning.

Joy or excitement, on the other hand, can manifest physically as a burst of energy or a pleasurable warmth in the stomach.

3.) You can also try the following exercise:

    a. Set either your smart phone or a timer so that it will sound off a discreet alarm at various points throughout the day.

b. Whenever the timer goes off, step away from whatever you are doing and then breathe in deeply a few times.

c. Take note of how you feel at that moment and notice how the sensation feels like physically. Give the said emotion a proper name (e.g., contentment, frustration, resignation, calmness, etc.).

d. The more you practice this exercise, the easier it becomes to recognize the variety of emotions that you may experience throughout the day.

4.) Keep a journal. Use it to note down how you feel in the morning upon waking, how you feel at various points throughout the day (via the previously-mentioned exercise), how you feel at night before you go off to sleep, and any other significant feeling that may arise at any point.

It is also important to note that it is possible for anyone to feel a mix of emotions as well. For example, you can feel happy and thrilled for a child who is off to college yet a little sad and anxious for him or her to be setting off from home for the first time.

Whatever it is you may feel, allow yourself to ride out all the emotions fully, and then take stock of them in your journal.

5.) Browse through your journal from time to time. This allows you to do two things. One is that it can help you gain a better understanding of how you feel about something when you are faced with an event or a situation that may have occurred in the past, allowing you to benefit from your previous insights.

6.) It also helps you spot on emotional patterns so that you can wield better control over your behavior and thus behave in a way that is more apt to the situation.

Another benefit is that it helps you see how far you have come in your journey towards self-awareness and self-control. This part is especially important on days when you may need a bit more of encouragement to continue your progress.

NOTES:

CHAPTER 3:
BE AWARE OF YOUR BEHAVIOR

Once you have become better aware of your emotions, it is time to cultivate the same level of awareness where your behavior is concerned.

In the same way that the mind and body are linked inextricably, your emotions often have more bearing on your actions in more ways than you might realize. Knowing how certain kinds of emotions affect certain aspects of your daily life, such as how productive you are or how well you communicate with others, is a crucial part of exerting more control over your behavior.

1.) Begin with not attaching any labels to your behavior just yet. Refrain from labeling a reaction as a good or bad sort, at least at the beginning. It is far easier to be honest with yourself when you are not passing judgment on your emotional actions and reactions.

2.) Practice tuning in to your knee-jerk reactions to everyday situations. What do your default reactions say about your emotional state in a situation? Be on the lookout especially for strong emotions that bring on certain kinds of behavioral impulses. The more you are able to understand the sort of emotions that bring on these impulses, the higher your EQ will be and the better you will get at controlling your actions in the future.

Some of the more common examples of behavioral impulses are as follows:

a. Strong feelings of anger and frustration can compel most people to shout, raise their voices, or even stomp their feet out of irritation. If you are of the less vocal sort, you might find yourself simply walking out on someone or something when you are angry.

b. Insecurity or embarrassment can make you want to withdraw from social contact or scurry away from the scene to avoid any stares or whispers that may come your way.

Some people can react differently in the light of such feelings and end up trying to make themselves look more confident and less affected than they actually are to draw attention away from their own feelings of inadequacy.

c. When people feel overwhelmed either by despair or pleasure, they often get the urge to cry or to lose track of what they were occupied with up until the object or situation stimulating the said emotion came along.

d. Bursts of joy or excitement from a piece of good news often make you break out into a grin or a giggle.

   Some people are even made chatty and giddy by the said feelings while quite a few retreat into themselves to better process their good fortune.

3.) End each day by recording your emotions and actions into your journal. As mentioned in the previous chapter, you can also use your emotions journal as a log for your daily behavioral observations.

   As with your emotions, strive to see a common pattern in your behavior as well.

For example, do you tend to bottle up your emotions and behave in a normal and predictable fashion even when faced with something or someone that either irritates or thrills you to no end?

Or are you less restrained with your reactions altogether? Do you laugh, cry, or shout angrily as you see fit rather than leaving the other person guessing about what you are truly feeling in a given moment?

Again, regardless of which pattern your typical behavior resembles more, do not apply any judgment.

4.) See if there are any behavioral patterns that you do wish to improve on or enhance. There really isn't a particular right or wrong behavioral pattern to follow, only one that works better for you and the ones around you.

If you work in a place where solitude and silence is prized for instance, then you may want to be more subdued with regards to your reactions and behavior.

On the other hand, if you wish to feel better connected to an especially gregarious family or group of friends, then you might determine that you need to work on being a bit more demonstrative with your emotions.

Once you become more aware of how your emotions impact your actions and how you tend to be behave in certain situations, the easier it is to settle on how you should act in a certain scenario or in daily life altogether.

NOTES:

CHAPTER 4:
TAKE RESPONSIBILITY FOR YOURSELF

Once you are better acquainted with both your feelings and behavior, then it is time for the third and perhaps the most challenging step towards a higher EQ and better self-control: taking responsibility.

It is important to take responsibility for your feelings and actions because while they may be triggered by something or someone, you alone are entirely responsible for them. This is because your feelings and actions come from you and from no one else.

You are not responsible for how another person behaves, but you are responsible for how you react to his or her behavior. If, say, another person were to insult or criticize you and you lashed out at that person in response, then you alone are to blame for lashing out.

Whatever the other person said or did to elicit such a reaction from you, s/he did not make the decision to react in that way. You did, and you should never lose sight of that.

Taking responsibility for your thoughts and actions do not just give you accountability, but it also provides you with a purpose.

Once you have fully accepted that all of your reactions and feelings are entirely within your control, the easier it will be for you to practice restraint and moderation whenever such is required.

To make it easier for you to do this step, there are some things that you can bear in mind:

1.) Understand how you alone are responsible for how you feel about certain things. While most people are convinced that some things or some people can stir certain emotions in them, the truth is that you cannot be made to feel sad, happy, ashamed, or upset without your consent. To believe otherwise is to mislead yourself.

2.) Attempt to comprehend how you come to experience feeling certain emotions. Often, your reactive emotions are determined by two things: your life experience and how you understood a certain interaction.

For example, analyze the possible ways in which you can react to an insult from someone.

Basically, you will either feel sad and/or angry or you may feel completely apathetic or perhaps even amused. What determines the emotion you end up feeling then?

Say, your father was the one who called you stupid or foolish. Chances are, this sort of remark would sting. However, if the insult came from a homeless person on the street, then you would probably just brush it off and forget about it.

To understand how the two situations brought about completely different reactions, look at your interpretation of the remark, the significance you assign to it, and the context in which it was said.

The interpretation is pretty straightforward: that you must have committed a foolish mistake.

The significance that you choose to attach to the resulting insult is where all the difference lies. In the first case, the insulting remark has great significance because it came from your father, someone whom you most likely have a great deal of respect and admiration for.

Thus, you are probably keen to have his approval and the opposite inevitably makes you upset.

In the second case, the homeless person is a complete stranger and is perhaps someone whose circumstances do not inspire much admiration or respect.

Thus, such an insult coming from someone who appears to be beneath you in some way is hardly deemed worthy of a deep emotional response.

Therefore, be a keen student of recognizing when a remark, be it an insult or praise, should be worthy of significance.

After all, why should you allow yourself to feel put out just because your hairdresser (who most likely profits from your repeated visits to the salon) thinks that your hair color makes you look peaky when your significant other finds you highly attractive no matter what?

3.) Recognize your own mistakes and shortcomings, and own up to them. This is incredibly difficult as it takes a certain degree of humility and recognition of one's own inadequacies.

However difficult it may seem, it is still far preferable to the alternatives, which is to either ignore your mistakes (and thus miss the opportunity to learn from them and to better yourself) or to bluff and bluster your way through things to hide your inadequacies (a move that is unlikely to help you build strong bonds with others).

NOTES:

CHAPTER 5:
RESPOND RATHER THAN REACT

At this point in the game, the key is being proactive rather than reactive. Once you have a solid understanding of your own emotions and are able to accept responsibility for them, you can then turn your attentions towards the sort of behavioral patterns associated with people who have high EQ.

Again, you have no control over what happens to you and over the kind of emotions that the people in your life could trigger in you but you do have control over what happens in you.

How you process a situation, identify the emotion it brings about and decide whether or not (and how to) re-act on it.

One thing that you need to grasp in the journey towards better self-control is that there is a small but significant difference between reacting and responding.

To react to something or to someone is to relieve or express an emotion in response to a certain trigger.

This sort of action is often unconscious and perhaps even impulsive in nature, such as yelling or swearing at someone who inadvertently cut you off on the road while you are rushing towards an important meeting.

Responding, on the other hand, entails acknowledging the emotion you've felt and then making a decision about your next move before executing it.

Unlike reactions, where you behave based on an unconscious impulse, a response involves a conscious deliberation.

To make light of the example in the previous paragraph, rather than swearing and yelling at the person who cut you off on the road, you could simply decide to take a few deep breaths to vent your frustration and then concentrate on the next opportunity to swap lanes.

There are ways you can practice developing a responsive mode of behavior rather than a reactive one, and these include the following:

1.) Refrain from acting on impulse, but acknowledge any emotions that may arise just the same. When you are confronted with something that makes you sad or angry, allow yourself a moment to fully feel the emotion.

This is akin to telling yourself that you acknowledge what has happened and how it made you feel. Doing so makes it easier to subsequently let go of the said emotion.

Note that this also applies to positive emotions like joy or excitement as a responsive action rather than a reactive one will prevent you from making any potentially troublesome promises or decisions in the heat of the moment.

1.) Once the first wave of emotion has passed, make a firm decision about how you would like to behave. This is where developing a strong sense of self-control would kick in.

Rather than giving in to your emotions and lashing out, think about how you would prefer to behave in the situation and muster up your sense of control to keep yourself firmly on that path.

For instance, when faced with someone who is interrupting while you are in the middle of something, take a moment to collect yourself before calmly expressing how this is not a good time for you rather than simply snapping at them to leave you alone.

2.) Follow the ten-second rule. Before making a decision on how to act (especially when faced with a particularly strong emotion such as anger or excitement), pause for ten seconds first.

3.) Direct your thoughts to a mental countdown while taking deep, steadying breaths before you allow your thoughts to return to the situation at hand.

By then, you will most likely be calmer and thus better able to think of a more desirable response.

NOTES:

CHAPTER 6:
WORK ON YOUR CONNECTIONS
CONNECT WITH OTHER PEOPLE

Being in tune with your emotions, thoughts, and actions is but half of a good EQ equation. The other half has to do with the ability to formulate good connections with other people.

So, how does being empathetic towards other people improve your self-control? For one, heightened empathy towards others is a sign of a mature and well-developed EQ, and a good sense of self-control is always a part of that package.

Another reason is because you are far less likely to behave impulsively towards or against someone when you have a good grasp of why they behave or react in the way that they do. Empathy often goes hand in hand with a more considerate outlook towards people, and this form of compassion often does wonders for anyone's self-control.

Given that, what sort of things can you do to help you connect with other people better?

1.) Cultivate an open mind. Most of the conflicts between people often occur because of ignorance and a refusal to compromise or even to hear the other person out. A person with a low EQ is often quick to argue with someone on the sole basis that the latter just doesn't share the same viewpoint.

To curb this impulse and to help yourself develop the ability to deal with conflicts in a calmer and more controlled manner, keep your mind open to new possibilities, even if they might go against some of your most deeply-ingrained beliefs.

You do not have to change your viewpoint, but you do have to attempt to see the merit in the other side's opinions.

As an exercise, listen to debates on the radio or watch out for them on the television. Regardless of which side of the debate you fall on, listen to each argument that comes up and point out the merits in each one.

2.) Cliché as it may sound, try to put yourself in the other person's shoes. Instead of feeling put off when someone does not react emotionally as you would, marvel at how they respond and try to analyze why they behave that way.

Try to think about how the other person's experiences and struggles can be quite different from your own, and how this plays into how differently they behave or react as opposed to you.

3.) Be truly present in your conversations with other people. Rather than letting your thoughts drift away elsewhere while a friend or family member recounts a story about how their day went, focus your attention on what they are saying.

Ask questions and occasionally reiterate some key things they may have mentioned to make it clear that you are fully participating in the conversation.

Not only will this make the other person feel a stronger bond with you but it will also give you some insights into what makes the other person tick.

4.) Talk to someone you normally wouldn't have a conversation with. This is one way of challenging your own biases and preconceived assumptions and thus raising your EQ.

If there is someone at work or at home that you don't especially get along with, find time to engage them in a light, casual conversation.

Better yet, try talking to at least one stranger every week, preferably someone of a different race, social status, or educational background from you.

You may be quite surprised at how just about anyone has something important to teach you and at how the experience could inspire you to suspend your biases and judgment when you meet someone similar next time.

NOTES:

CHAPTER 7:
DEVELOP A POSITIVE ATTITUDE

Ultimately, people find themselves drawn to a person with a healthy EQ since s/he tends to espouse a positive outlook on life, regardless of the circum-stances.

Everyone regardless of their station in life is bound to run into problems, disappointments, and frustrations, so the ability to cultivate a positive environment is always a skill that is worthy of cultivation.

After all, what is the point of developing an enviable EQ when you don't take time to notice how far you've come and to savor the feeling of accomplished a significant amount of progress?

Often, achieving great things in life is impossible without a healthy degree of optimism. Endeavors like writing a book or establishing a business are often faced with unfavorable odds.

So the ability to maintain a positive vision of what you wish to achieve often fuels how much self-control you can exert in the face of challenges, chief among them is the temptation to just throw in the towel.

Cultivating a positive environment and mindset is not only beneficial for your EQ, but it also does wonders for your physical and mental health as well.

As a bonus, optimism can be quite contagious, so it can also do a world of good to the people around you.

To nurture a positive attitude, you can try any of the following tips:

1.) Train yourself to see opportunities rather than problems. Many of the world's greatest inventions and businesses were built to provide a solution to a problem or two.

It has even been said that problems are merely opportunities dressed up in work clothes, and anyone who manages to adopt such a perspective would benefit greatly from it.

In most problematic situations, there is always something constructive that can be done. For example, if you happen to be stuck in traffic, you can use the time to brush up on your audio language lessons rather than bemoan how the set-up is delaying you from your appointments.

2.) Use the power of humor to get through tough times. Listen to a gifted comedian's take on a particular life problem, and allow yourself to see the humor in it and to laugh.

Laughing and smiling are two of the most effective stress busters and they can often allow you to see things in a different light afterwards.

If you have trouble finding something funny or laughable in a situation, you can find a friend who does and end up forging a strong bond in the process.

3.) Read or consume inspirational material. A wise man once said that inspiration is much like bathing in the sense that you need it every day to keep yourself fresh. To keep yourself inspired and motivated, pick up some quality reading materials.

A good biography of a person who inspires you is a good place to start, as is a well-written self-help book that is meant to change your mind set in a certain way.

If you aren't too keen on reading, you can opt to watch inspirational videos or tune in to the keynote speeches of famous men and women who overcame a great deal of adversity in order to achieve success in their chosen fields.

4.) Keep yourself in good company. Hang around people who exhibit the same kind of attitude that you want to see in yourself.

Spend more time with friends who will always encourage and support you, and can tell you about how they prevail over their own everyday struggles to find that silver lining. Eventually, their sunny dose of optimism is bound to rub off on you somehow.

NOTES:

CHAPTER 8:
FULLY COMMIT

The development of a healthy emotional intelligence is the work of a lifetime. It is unlike a skill or trade that you can learn once and then drop.

Given that human nature is highly changeable and is subject to all sorts of events that may happen over the course of a lifetime, you will constantly be coming up with new ways to address new challenges and emotions.

Thus, even when you feel as though you have fully mastered the contents of this book and its applications, you should still remember to keep practicing the steps therein.

Constant improvement is the name of the game, and the ability to commit is one that will get you very far here.

Should you need more concrete steps that will keep you committed and focused, the following are good examples of such:

1.) Come up with new goals for yourself. Once you have accomplished your desired level of self-control, set your sights on another aspect of your personality that could benefit from improvement.

Perhaps you may wish to relate better to other people or to work on your leadership skills? Whatever you choose, it is important to keep striving for improvement.

2.) Use your journal to keep track of your progress. Even when you feel more in control of your emotions and actions, you should still maintain the practice of writing in your journal.

During the times when you might feel stuck or listless, open up your journal and see how your journey towards a healthier EQ has greatly improved the way you process emotions and respond to certain situations.

3.) Take on a protégé. Once you reach a certain EQ level, there are bound to be people in your inner circle who will notice the improvement in your personality and they could very well be keen to do the same for themselves.

Find someone who can benefit from your example and spend time with them in consultation as they would see fit. Not only will this foster good will with others, but it will also help you to remember the key lessons you have learned so far whenever you have to impart them to someone else.

4.) Don't be too hard on yourself. Refrain from comparing your progress to that of other people's and compete with no one but your past self.

Recognize that there will be bad days and good days, and that how well you deal with the former can only propel you even further in the journey towards your best self.

Remember to celebrate your progress from time to time and to savor just how far you have come in your efforts to improve yourself.

CONCLUSION

Thank you again for downloading this book!

I am confident that this book was able to help you gain a better understanding of the concept of emotional intelligence and how healthy levels of it can help you, to realize a happier and more accomplished life.

The next step is to apply what you have learned from this book and to reap the benefits that accompany your progress.

TO DO LIST / NOTES

1.

2.

3.

4.

5.

6.

7.

PRIORITIES:

A FEW WORDS FROM THE AUTHOR: E.N. RICHARDSON

„Dear Reader of this book. Thank You! For your support and trust – buying this book! I really hope that I was able to help you with some major improvement technques.

Stay on your path of Self-Improvement. I experienced myself what a great impact this can have on your future.

I once read a quote from someone that I carry with me and that I want to share with you:

'If you are willing to do the work –
You can Have Anything!'
_ unknown author

You bought this book – this shows that you are willing to do the work. You are ahead of so many other people because, most people only want to improve and succeed, but are not willing to do whatever it takes to achieve it! Keep working on yourself!

If you need more valuable tips to improve yourself take a look at my other books down below! Or visit my authors page on Amazon here: **E. N. Richardson**
All the best for you!

I highly appreciate your support by leaving a Review on Amazon here.
This really helps!

Yours"

E. N. Richardson

A FEW WORDS FROM THE PUBLISHER:
BE-TO-CE _ PUBLISHING

We are very proud working together with bestselling author E.N. Richardson and want to thank him for – publishing his fourth book in the upcoming days with us!

Please support the author by giving a good Review here: *Review on Amazon*

If you love free books: We want to thank you for your trust, becoming one of our customers and friends. We send out our Newsletter on a regular basis with Free Books from our portfolio for our valued customers.

Just **Sign in** and **Watch out** for the next free books rolling to your inbox.

<<<< Subscribe Here >>>>

http://j.mp/FreeBooksList

<u>**On the next Pages for You:**</u>

Some of our actual Book-Recommendations.

Books about Love, Communication,

Relationships and becoming – "a better You!"

UNDERSTANDING MEN
AN ENTERTAINING GUIDE TO
FINDING, ATTRACTING AND KEEPING
MR. RIGHT!

Stop Dreaming about Your Perfect Relationship! Get   it!

The Experiment! What will a book be like, when the Relationship Coach James Kingsley(♂), starts to discuss his Inside Knowledge about Men – with a confident, open-minded and witty woman?

You will know: 'How Men Think'. 'What really attracts Men' and 'What you can do to make him really want You and - Never(!) Let You Go again!' *And laugh your brains out – by the way!*

Learn the Secrets, most Women - will never know!

<u>Limited Time Offer:</u> Check on Amazon

GUIDE TO EASY COMMUNICATION HOW TO WIN FRIENDS AND MASTER TO LEAD CONVERSATIONS.

Communication is Key - Everywhere in Life!

Rock-solid advice that carried thousands of people up the ladder of success:

- Boost Your Relationships & Make people like You
- How to win people to think your way
- How to never run out of words again
- How to change peoples behavior – the smart way

Check on Amazon for Communication + E.N. Richardson

POWERFUL MINDSET TRICKS
CREATE A HAPPY AND SUCCESSFUL FUTURE!
GAIN THE THINGS YOU WANT IN LIFE!

What you Think, you Become!

Learn in 21 practical Lessons how to boost Your Happiness & Success!

Section I: Change Your Mindset Toward Yourself
Section II: Change Your Mindset Toward Others
Section III: Become a better You!
Section IV: Change Your Money Mindset

- **Check on Amazon – Mindset +** + E.N. Richardson

EMOTIONAL INTELLIGENCE (EQ)
7 EFFECTIVE METHODS & EQ SECRETS!
LEVERAGE YOUR SUCCESS & HAPPINESS!

Simple Life Changer!

Release Your Power of Emotional Intelligence
1. Understand Yourself and Others Better
2. Improve Your Success in Managing Your Relationships
3. proven for Business and Private
4. 7 effective methods to Master your Emotional Intelligence

- Check on Amazon –
Search: Emotional Intelligence + + E.N. Richardson

THE ESCAPE-PLAN
OVERCOME ANXIETY, DEPRESSION & ANGER!
BOOST HAPPINESS, CONFIDENCE & YOUR LIFE!

Conquer Anxiety, Depression & Anger. Advice from someone, who has been there - and ESCAPED!

Section I: Limiting The Negatives
- Overcoming Anxiety / Defeating Fear
- Coping With Depression / Outdoing Anger
Section II: Increasing The Positive
- Allowing Happiness In Your Life
- Start to live with more ease –Love what you do!
- Creating Confidence / Being Moved By Motivation

Check on Amazon **/ Self Help +** + E.N. Richardson

E.N. Richardson

This document is geared towards providing exact and reliable information in regards to the topic and issue covered. The publication is sold with the idea that the publisher is not required to render accounting, officially permitted, or otherwise, qualified services. If advice is necessary, legal or professional, a practiced individual in the profession should be ordered.

From a Declaration of Principles which was accepted and approved equally by a Committee of the American Bar Association and a Committee of Publishers and Associations.

The information provided herein is stated to be truthful and consistent, in that any liability, in terms of inattention or otherwise, by any usage or abuse of any policies, processes, or directions contained within is the solitary and utter responsibility of the recipient reader. Under no circumstances will any legal responsibility or blame be held against the publisher for any reparation, damages, or monetary loss due to the information herein, either directly or indirectly.

Respective authors own all copyrights not held by the publisher.

The information herein is offered for informational purposes solely, and is universal as so. The presentation of the information is without contract or any type of guarantee assurance.

The trademarks that are used are without any consent, and the publication of the trademark is without permission or backing by the trademark owner. All trademarks and brands within this book are for clarifying purposes only and are the owned by the owners themselves, not affiliated with this document.